Cold

COLD READING AND HOW TO BE GOOD AT IT

Basil Hoffman

Dramaline Publications

Printed in the United States of America.

Dramaline Publications
36-851 Palm View Road
Rancho Mirage, CA 92270
Phone 760/770-6076 Fax 760/770-4507
E-Mail: drama@cyberg8t.com

Library of Congress Cataloging-in-Publication Data

Hoffman, Basil
Cold reading and how to be good at it/Basil Hoffman
p. cm.
ISBN 0-940669-42-0 (alk. paper)
1. Acting—Auditions. 2. Acting—Vocational guidance. I. Title.
PN2071.A92 H58 1999
792'.028—dc21 98-52463

Cover design by John Sabel

This book is printed on acid-free paper, a paper that meets the requirements of the American Standard of Permanence of paper for printed library material.

CONTENTS

(*contents cont'd.*)

(*contents, cont'd.*)

(*contents cont'd.*)

PREFACE

More than thirty-five years in the acting business in New York and Los Angeles have provided me with more than ample experience as a basis for my conclusions about cold reading. All of the information contained herein is based upon my observations about the things that work and the things that don't work, not only in the process of preparing and performing cold readings, but also in the way an actor relates emotionally to the process.

Thousands of auditions and more than 400 professional acting jobs of my own, coupled with the countless auditions and acting jobs performed by the professional actors I coach, have been and continue to be the basis for my observations. All of the ideas in this book are intended to improve the actor's cold reading skills and to develop and reinforce a constructive mental approach to the cold reading process. I offer them because I know they work. They have worked for me, and they have worked for many others. I don't claim that my conclusions are rules, because I don't know if they are rules. I only know they work.

I have chosen a question-and-answer format for this book because it seemed to be the best way to cover the subject. Most of the questions are questions I have been asked in seminars and coaching sessions. Those that were not asked should have been. I have answered all of them with an intent to be truthful and constructive. Every question I answer is a question that needs to be answered. All of the information I have provided is important. Some of it is vital. If you disagree with my conclusions, give them a second thought before you discard them. They have been formed after very careful consideration, and they have been proven correct in practical application at the highest levels of this industry.

In this book (and in the industry), the terms "reading" and "cold reading" are used interchangeably. Regarding my use of the words "he," "him," and "his" in the context of the dictionary definition, "one whose sex is unknown or immaterial," no other words would have been both grammatical and all-inclusive. I frequently use the words "they," "them," and "their" to refer to the various casting directors, writers, directors, producers, studio executives, and network executives for whom actors perform cold readings.

The casting process for on-camera television commercials is different from theater, film, and television casting in a number of important ways. The final section is devoted to those differences. No reference is made to voice acting, only because the principles of acting and cold reading to which this book is devoted are not applicable to that industry.

BASIL HOFFMAN

INTRODUCTION

What is a cold reading?

First, it is important to know what a cold reading is not. A cold reading is not a "cold" reading. No actor in a professional situation is ever asked to read from material that he has not prepared. And you must never do it. Never.

In fact, if a cold reading is to be successful, it must be a "warm" reading. It must have the warmth of life. Even when you have only a few minutes to prepare, you must find the real person in the role. Ideally, the person you find will be the one who satisfies the demands of the script, and not the one who satisfies the needs of your ego.

Why is this book necessary?

This book is necessary because cold reading is the process by which most professional acting jobs are filled, and it is in every actor's best interest to know as much as he can about it. To succeed in the business of acting, most actors will need to master a cold reading technique so that it becomes reliable and natural. Some actors will develop an effective technique on their own. Many will not. For the actor who is not comfortable with the cold reading process, there are only two options: get lucky or get help.

Unfortunately, until now, the actor who needed help with his understanding of, and approach to, cold reading has had limited dependable means for working through his problem to a successful solution. Books that seem to offer the promise of cold reading instruction have generally fallen short in two critical areas—they are not specific and they are not authoritative. First, the book on cold reading must explain *how to do it.* Second, it must be written by someone *who has done it successfully hundreds of times.* This is that book.

BEING A PROFESSIONAL ACTOR

What are the three essentials of professionalism?

The acting profession makes only three *demands* of its members. Those demands are so fundamental as prerequisites to success, especially in collaborative endeavors, that they must apply to most other professions as well. The three essentials are promptness, preparedness, and propriety. If you are deficient in any one of the three, some aspect of the work will suffer. Another characteristic of all three conditions is that they are each indicators of self-respect and respect for the rights of others.

Promptness is the first indicator of reliability—are you dependable? They need to know that you will be there when they need you. Tardiness will not inspire their confidence. The other part of promptness is personal and emotional. Every business appointment you ever have should be used to develop and reinforce relationships, which have an important emotional component. Your ability (or inability) to be prompt will have a major effect on the emotional response to you—how comfortable they are with you and how much they want to work with you. Professional behavior will make them like you, and the easiest part of that is being on time. Nobody you ever meet in the business will be unimportant enough to be kept waiting. As a practical matter, your being late may cost them money. Nobody likes that.

Preparedness indicates a work ethic. Your preparedness for a reading is an accurate predictor of your preparedness on the set. Even if you are absolutely perfect for the part, you may lose it in the reading if they foresee that your lack of readiness will cause them production problems later on. Giving a reading that indicates an understanding and command of the script and the character is an absolute necessity. Failing in that, no other factor will convince them to hire you.

Propriety (or the lack of it) has a significant effect on the image of you that is transmitted to everyone who encounters you, even on the most superficial levels. Propriety means appropriateness, in every sense. It means speaking appropriately, dressing appropriately, and behaving appropriately in every situation. Propriety demands self-awareness at all times, particularly for people who are inclined toward impulses of inappropriate behavior. Propriety is expected of actors because propriety is expected of everyone. Unfortunately, some famous actors get a lot of news coverage for their lack of propriety, while the vast majority of more important actors get no coverage for behaving themselves. Also, there are no news reports on the countless actors who have misbehaved themselves out of careers and out of the business. Of course, giving some attention to propriety will achieve one other important thing for you. It will make you a better person.

CASTING SITUATIONS

What is a general interview?

A general interview is an actor's meeting, usually with a casting director, with the primary purpose of introducing the actor to a casting director who is unfamiliar with his work, even though there may be no particular role or project appropriate for the actor at that time. General interviews are mutually beneficial since casting directors need to meet new actors, and actors need to be known by every casting director.

What is an interview?

Television commercial auditions in Los Angeles are called "interviews." The term is rarely used in any other way to describe an actor's interaction with others in the industry.

What is an audition?

Any performance an actor gives for the sole purpose of gaining future employment may be called an audition. Most appropriately a theatrical term, it has become commonly used in the film, television, and commercial industries as well.

What is a prereading?

A prereading is a screening reading. It is conducted by someone who cannot give the actor a job. The casting director's purpose in prereading an actor is to discern the actor's level of expertise and his suitability for the role for which he is reading. The actor's incentive for prereading is the expectation that it will result in a reading for someone who can actually hire him for the part.

Casting is an integral, vital function in the preproduction process. The success of every play, movie, and television show depends on casting. Because of the responsibility with which they are charged, most casting directors are skilled, and often creative, professionals who use the screening reading as an effective means for introducing new talent into the work pool. In recent years, however, new and inexperienced casting personnel have begun to misuse the prereading as a substitute for learning the essentials of the industry. In those cases, well-known actors are requested for prereadings because the casting person hasn't taken the time to review the actor's work or doesn't have the critical ability to assess what he has seen. An actor with a substantial body of work who is asked to preread should offer his demo tape instead. To me, the most succinct response to professional ignorance was delivered by two-time Academy Award winning director Fred Zinnemann (*From Here to Eternity* and *A Man For All Seasons*) when, in his seventies, he was being interviewed by a young, self-important studio production executive. When asked to supply a brief summary of his training and experience, Zinnemann replied, "You first."

What is a reading?

A reading is an unmemorized performance delivered to an audience of prospective employers for the purpose of getting an acting job in film or television.

What is a meeting?

A meeting is an audition without the performance. An actor who is asked to "meet" with a director or producer is usually not asked to review the material and will not be asked to read. In most cases when an actor attends a meeting his reputation has preceded him, and there is already a high level of interest in him for the role.

In the film and television industries all business appointments that are not readings are called meetings.

THE MATERIAL

What is a script?

A script is the full text of the show (play, teleplay, screenplay). Since scripts are subject to frequent rewrites prior to the completion of production (in film or television) or before opening night (of a play), scripts are always dated to indicate which revision they represent. In film and television, successive rewrites appear on different colored pages for easy identification.

What are sides?

In theater, sides are pages of the script containing only one character's dialogue, with a few words of the cue preceding each speech. Theatrical sides are used for learning lines.

In film and television, pages of selected scenes are called sides. Film and television sides are used as audition material and as a guide to each day's shooting schedule.

What is copy?

Scripts for radio and television commercials are called copy.

What is a cue card?

A cue card is a large sheet of poster board with lines of dialogue printed on it. Television actors and news reporters once used cue cards instead of memorizing or reading from scripts, but that use has been supplanted by electronic prompters. In recent years, cue cards have become widely used in the television commercial industry as an audition tool.

What is a story board?

A story board is an artist's cartoon-style, scene-by-scene depiction of a film, television, or commercial script. Commercial casting directors provide story boards to actors who are preparing to audition.

What is "the material?"

"The material" is the script or any part of a script that is supplied to an actor to prepare him for a reading.

GETTING THE READING

How do I get general interviews and readings?

Your ability to get general interviews and readings will be a good indication of the correctness of your overall approach to the acting profession. Meetings and readings are the only direct link to employment as an actor. Since your success will be determined by your employment, the first steps on your road to success will be the steps you take to get meetings and readings. So the question might more appropriately be, "Who hires actors, and how do I meet those people?"

To begin with, it is important for you to know who doesn't hire actors. Since your first step to employment is getting readings, you don't want to divert your energy and focus from that task in the pursuit of people who don't have readings to offer. In the industry, those people are called agents and managers. The function of agents and managers is to help you develop and maximize your career, not to start one for you. You must do the work to get your career started, before you begin hiring employees to help you. If you work correctly, you will get a career started, and it will begin to happen sooner than you think.

So, who hires actors? The answer is producers, directors, and, sometimes, casting directors. But casting directors are the *only* people who set up appointments for general interviews and readings, so your goal is to meet casting directors.

The best indirect way to meet casting directors is by appearing in plays and showcases attended by casting directors. It is an indirect method because you have no personal contact with them, but if your role is substantial and you are good in it, you will have made a positive impression. You must, however, follow up your performance with a phone call to request a general interview. It is personal contacts that build business relationships.

There are two direct approaches to meeting casting directors. One not very cost-effective approach is to enroll in a workshop taught by a casting director. It is an expensive approach because you will spend a considerable amount of money for one session, or a series of sessions, and meet only one casting director. And there are more than a hundred for you to meet. The most cost-effective and efficient way to meet casting directors is to call them on the phone and request general interviews, exactly the way you would do it if you were starting any other business with a new product to sell.

Some actors submit themselves for roles without ever meeting the casting directors, by obtaining casting information (sometimes unlawfully) on their own, and then sending their pictures and resumes to the casting directors in the same way that agents and managers do. But an actor who is not known by the casting director will not get a reading appointment as readily as an actor who is known. Make the effort to build those relationships.

You must work to get work. The only place where success comes before work is in the dictionary.

GETTING THE MATERIAL

How do I get the material?

After you have been hired, the script (and subsequent changes) will be delivered to you. For auditions, you may pick up the material at the casting office or studio, or you may have it faxed to you (or your agent, if you have one) for a small fee. Sometimes the studio will fax the material for no charge. In some instances, agents will get the material for their clients.

When can I get the material?

Usually the material is available as soon as the actor is given the audition appointment. It is to the actor's advantage to obtain the material as soon as it becomes available.

Can I get more material than they offer me?

Frequently, yes. For major roles, casting offices usually provide complete scripts, and in those instances no more material is available. Casting offices typically offer only sides to actors reading for supporting roles, but a simple request of a casting person may yield a complete script. Sometimes, when scripts aren't available to take out, an actor is permitted to read the script in the casting office.

PREPARATION—
UNDERSTANDING THE AUDITION PROCESS

Who will be in the audition room?

If the reading isn't videotaped, there will be, at the very least, one casting director and one director or producer. There might be a roomful: casting directors, director, producers, executive producers, writers, network and studio executives, and others. The actor will help his mental preparation by knowing in advance who he will be reading for.

What are they looking for?

They are never sure. If they knew, they would have hired that actor. There will be as many different concepts as there are people in the room.

How will I know which person in the audition room is the power person?

By looking in the mirror. The actor is always the power person in the audition. He is the only one who knows exactly who the character is.

How can I focus on getting the job?

You can't. Focus upon the character and his circumstances, and prepare to give the most truthful and interesting reading possible. Expending any energy at all toward the goal of getting the job is a waste of valuable rehearsal time, since getting the job is the only element of the reading process over which you have absolutely no control.

If your goal is to get the job, and you give a great reading but don't get hired, then your reading will have failed. If your goal is to give a great reading, and you give a great reading but don't get hired, your reading will have been successful. Don't give others the power to validate your work. If you do good, truthful, interesting work, you can expect the jobs to come. And they will come. If you focus on getting jobs, the rejections will destroy you.

You must be absolutely certain that the job is yours before you even read the script. Having that certainty will free you to give the best reading that it is possible to give.

Do they expect a performance in a cold reading?

Yes. Even if they say they don't. Despite the limited preparation time available and the likelihood that a desirable rehearsal space isn't available, producers and directors and casting directors do expect a performance in a cold reading. They may even believe that they don't. But they do.

If I give the best reading will I get the job?

Not necessarily. The best reading doesn't always get the job because so many other factors affect casting (some of these are the actor's eye color, hair color, sex, age, height, weight, ethnicity, persona, attitude, wardrobe, mannerisms, etc.) None of these factors alone will get you the job, but any one of them can lose the job. That is why the actor has to focus all his attention on the work. He has absolutely no control over the other stuff.

For a cold reading, how much time will I have to prepare?

Sometimes a week or more. Sometimes only a few minutes. It is to the producer's and the director's advantage to give the actor as much time as possible, but production schedules do not always cooperate, particularly in television. The actor has to make good use of whatever time he has. A good reading with short preparation time will inspire the confidence of the producer and director that the actor will perform well under pressure.

Is there a difference between reading for plays, movies, and television?

The acting requirements are never different, so, in the acting sense, plays, movies and television are the same. You must always be aware, however, of where the people for whom you are reading have placed themselves. Be sure that they see every facial expression and hear every word, and that they believe what they see and hear.

Projection should never be an issue, because projection is a mechanical concept, and acting is not. Natural human speech proceeds naturally from thoughts, always being heard when it is necessary to be heard. When it is necessary for the character to be heard, his intentions will propel his voice as much as is necessary. If the process by which you make your voice louder is mechanical, the resulting sound will be mechanical.

Beware of the fake intimacy trap. When speech is described as "soft," "gentle," or "intimate," it is *never* intended to be breathy. Breathy or whispered speech is not intimate speech. Nor is it real speech. Real, live human beings never carry on conversation in whispers, and when actors do it, the falseness is deafening. Words such as "soft," "gentle," and "intimate," when applied to speech, always refer to an intention of speech, and not to a sound level. Live truthfully in the material, and the sound will take care of itself.

When I worked with Peter Falk in "Columbo," we had a scene between the two of us that started in a doorway. Because of some logistics of microphone placement and our height difference, my voice wasn't being recorded as efficiently as Peter's. Sam Wanamaker, the director, asked me to speak louder. Peter said, "Sam, let me talk to Basil for a minute." So Peter took me aside to explain the sound situation to me, and this is what he said: "Basil, you're doing just great. We'll keep doing what we do, and make them do what they do." So Peter and I kept getting the acting right, and the sound department finally got the sound right. Peter Falk's point was clear. Don't do artificial things and expect them to come out real. It doesn't work in movies and television, and it doesn't work on the stage. It's all the same.

What is camera acting, or "acting for the camera"?

I have no idea. The concept makes as little sense as "acting for the audience." Acting is acting. Period.

When acting on camera, an actor should always be aware of the size of the frame and how much of him is supposed to be in it. Generally speaking, the smaller the frame, the more restricted an actor will be in his physical movement. In production, the actor can help himself enormously by ensuring that he hasn't ruined his own best take with a gesture or other movement that renders the shot unusable. Learning to control the blinking reflex is also helpful. The only other piece of camera information critical to the actor is the eyeline. The closer the shot, the more important it is for the actor to know where he must look in order to match the other shots. None of the technical requirements of the camera have anything to do with acting, any more than blocking on a stage has anything to do with acting. Staying in the frame and staying on the stage are parts of the same concept.

Camera awareness is relevant to an actor's cold reading preparation, because readings are frequently videotaped. In many cases, the director isn't present for the reading session, so the actor's taped performance will be the only thing the director sees. For that reason alone, the actor would be well advised to devote a lot of time to practicing reading off the page.

Should I memorize my lines for a reading?

Generally speaking, you should not memorize your lines, unless you have a photographic memory or there are so few lines that it is easier to play the scene or scenes without the script than with it.

Producers, directors, writers, and casting directors all know that the actor has had limited preparation time with the material when he comes in to read. They expect the actor to use the script. That is why the event is called a reading. An actor's ability to memorize lines is taken for granted. Their main concern is finding the right actor for the part.

Another reason not to memorize the lines, unless you can do it with absolutely no effort, is that it adds the pressure of memorization to your other, more important tasks in the reading. The words give a voice and a means of self-expression to the character. But if any part of your reading becomes about remembering lines, then the words will have actually become your enemy. You will have irreparably broken your own concentration and the concentration of everyone else in the room. Don't put that obstacle in your path. There is no point to it.

What are the two fundamental truths about every script?

The first thing you must be prepared to accept about every script, before you read one word, is that it is the best script ever written. Armed with that piece of irrefutable knowledge, you will be relieved of any impulse you might have had to waste valuable time and energy critiquing the material. You will be able to focus your attention directly on finding all the specific points of excellence. The expectation of quality will be the animating force in your approach to the material, and you will be inspired to bring that out of it. If you accept a lesser conception, the result will, of necessity, be less rewarding for you (and for your audience). You can only bring out of a script what is in it. You get to decide.

The other fact you must accept about every script you read is that it was written for you. Knowing that will eliminate any possibility that you might, even for a moment, imagine that some other actor could play your role. You will be free to explore the infinite possibilities of playing the part to its best advantage (and to yours as well), secure in the knowledge that every choice you make is the right choice because it is your role.

Having the best script ever written written for you gives you a tremendous advantage when you read for a part. It also places some responsibility on your shoulders to glorify the material in every way you can, and to be most reluctant to change it without having first investigated all the other options.

A word of caution: from a practical standpoint, every defect you perceive in a script creates an obstacle to your ability to give a good reading. Give yourself enough obstacles and a good reading will be impossible. Regarding the role, if you picture another actor playing the part, cancel your appointment—you're finished.

What is Situation Perception, why do I need to know about it, and how can it affect my reading?

Situation Perception is the term I use to describe the acting process. Situation Perception is the concept that isolates *all* the key elements of the acting experience. *Acting is Situation Perception.* Acting is not objective, because human behavior is not objective. Human behavior is based upon subjective perception, of the self and everything else in the universe. If acting were objective, it would be called reporting. But it isn't called reporting. It's called acting. *The reality in every acting situation is only what the character perceives it to be.*

You need to know about Situation Perception because your reading will fail proportionately to the number of essential elements of the acting experience that you disregard. Conversely, each of the elements that you incorporate into your work will make your reading richer and more compelling.

Situation Perception defines the acting experience by the following seven essential components:

1. WHO are you (who is the character)—age, health, state of mind, social condition, station in life—and how does that affect your feelings and your behavior?

2. WHAT is the event, and how does that affect your feelings and your behavior?

3. WHERE is the event—what nation, what region, indoors or outdoors, good weather or bad, public or private, formal or informal, familiar or unfamiliar, safe or dangerous—and how does that affect your feelings and your behavior?

4. WHY are you there (your reasons, not the reasons of others)—what do you expect to happen and what do you want to happen—and how does that affect your feelings and your behavior?

5. WHEN does the event take place—the year, the time of year, time of day, date of particular significance—and how does that affect your feelings and your behavior?

6. WHERE were you before the scene starts and where will you be after the scene ends, and how does that affect your feelings and your behavior?

7. WHO are the other people in the script, or referred to in the script, what do they say about you, how do they behave toward you, and how does that affect your feelings and your behavior?

Take the time to use the Situation Perception concept every time you prepare a reading. Your work will be more specific and powerful as a result.

What does the word "compass" mean when you use it in discussing a role or a performance?

I have adopted the word "compass" to denote the fullness or the totality of the character. The industry uses the word "arc" to describe the same thing. But it doesn't.

An arc, as defined in the dictionary, is a curve or a part of a circle. In other words, an arc is a shape but it lacks completeness. It is a good thing for your character to have a shape. It is a good thing for your reading or your performance to have a shape. But it is also absolutely necessary that they be complete.

The dictionary defines compass to mean "boundary, circumference, range, scope." It is also described as "the reach or extent of something." Since a compass contains all 360 degrees of a circle, there is nothing left out. A compass is all-encompassing. Just as a compass is complete, so is every character complete. Every role deserves completeness. It is the actor's job to find all the parts.

Readings, by their limits of time and space, place limitations on the actor's work. The actor, however, must never buy into those limitations by regarding the possibilities of the reading as limited or finite. The character you are playing is always a real person, and the possibilities of that are infinite, even in a limited space with limited time. Don't sell your character short because you're doing a reading, or for any other reason. Remember, you are the character, and you deserve better.

Will there be instances in which some elements of the character's situation won't need to be considered?

No. There will be elements that will seem to have little or no effect on your character's feelings and behavior. But you can't know that until you have considered them.

What is a character's "essence," and why is it important for me to identify it?

A character's essence is the fundamental core quality that is constantly projected. It is the force that ultimately motivates the character's every decision and action. The essence can usually be described by a single word, such as fearless, rigid, angry, methodical, suspicious, timid, violent, forthright, or nervous. The character's behavior in every situation is controlled by his essence.

It is important to identify the character's essence because every acting choice you make will depend on it. It will be the glue that holds your performance together in a cohesive characterization, regardless of the variety and severity of the character's conflicts, challenges, and personal demons. Your character's essence will determine, in large part, his posture, the way he walks, and his manner of speech. His essence is his permanent imprint. Because acting is subjective, different actors approaching the same part might apply different words to describe the essence of the character, and each description is correct if the logic of the description is supported by the material. There is a range of legitimate interpretations for every character, and each actor will perceive the character's essence to be the one that most closely approximates his own essence, unless the actor has the unusual ability to leave his ego out of the process. Some actors bend every character they play to the predilections of their own essences, even when those choices violate the sense of the material, and some of those actors have the good fortune to make careers out of it. I don't recommend that approach because Lady Luck isn't dependable.

Always find the character's essence in the logic of the material, and be sure it's something you can sustain truthfully and realistically with a small amount of preparation. And always make it an active (rather than passive) choice because active choices will make your work stronger and clearer.

Your character's essence should be apparent from the moment you enter the audition room until you leave.

Never drop out of it. Convince them that you are the character.

What is the difference between playing an attitude and playing a character (and are attitude and essence the same thing)?

Playing an attitude is a restrictive acting concept that predetermines a character's response in any given situation based on that one attitude. Even the most one-dimensional (seeming) character has many personality facets. This is *always* true. It is the actor's problem to find them.

Attitude and essence are not the same thing. One attitude is one attitude. The essence of a character is that dominant quality of personality from which all his attitudes are formed.

What does "living in the moment" mean and what is its importance?

Living in the moment is what human beings do *all the time.* The person you are playing behaves exactly in the same way. *Every moment.* The concept is vital to acting.

As an actor, you must accept as indisputable fact the idea that it is impossible to think or feel more than one thing in any one moment. Furthermore, it is absolutely necessary that your character live each moment only in the present. It is impossible to live past moments because they are gone, and impossible to live future moments because they don't exist yet.

No matter how confused or conflicted a character may be, each moment contains only one thing, and it must be a complete thing because the next moment will have its own life. A character involved in a love-hate relationship does not love and hate in the same moment; he loves in one moment and hates in the next. A character who can't make up his mind doesn't think two things in the same moment; he thinks one thing one moment and something else in the next moment.

Filling each moment with a single, complete idea will give your reading clarity. You will be forced into specific thinking, and, as a result, greater variety. In life, people's moments do not flow effortlessly and seamlessly into each other, and when you see it in a performance it always looks like acting. Let the person you are playing be a real person, living each moment as it comes. Wonderful, surprising things will happen.

How important is the element of surprise, and how can I get that into my reading?

The element of surprise in a reading (and, of course, in a performance) is very important, because it injects the truthfulness of unpredictable reality into the life of the character. If your life were a script, every page you turn to would be filled with revelations, and you would react appropriately, making adjustments all along the way. Some reactions and adjustments would be minor, because the events, though new, are neither consequential nor unfamiliar. Other events, however, would be so unexpected that your programmed behavior would be disturbed.

In Alan Pakula's film *Comes a Horseman,* I play George Bascomb, an eastern geologist whose boss, an oilman played by George Grizzard, wants drilling rights to property owned by two rival ranchers, played by Jane Fonda and Jason Robards. There is a scene in which I make a presentation to Jason Robards, and when I finish, the script has George Grizzard dismissing me from the meeting with a simple, "Thank you." I suggested to Alan Pakula that, even though the script says that I leave the room, I might not know that I'm supposed to leave. So Alan said, "Don't leave, and see what happens." As the scene appears in the film, I finish my presentation, George Grizzard says, "Thank you," and I sit down, proud and ready to take part in the rest of the meeting. Then George says, "Thank you. That will be all." It is only at that point that I realize that I was supposed to leave. So I am caught off guard, embarrassed and feeling foolish. The element of surprise makes the moment very real.

Every script is full of potential surprises. You have to look for them. Make your character work to have to fulfill his life. Your readings (and your acting) will be much richer for it.

Is there a difference between demonstrating and indicating?

Yes. One is truthful and the other is not.

Indicating is a product of objective perception instead of subjective perception. When an actor *thinks* a character should have a particular feeling (or lack of feeling) and shows the audience what he thinks, he is indicating. Besides its apparent falseness, indicating gets in the way of whatever might occur at that moment in the life of the character if the character were allowed to experience it. Indicating is sometimes called fake acting.

Demonstrating is showing what the character is actually experiencing, and it is a vital aspect of the acting process. Regardless of the honesty of the actor's work, that work is essentially worthless if it all stays inside the character. Everything must be demonstrated, even a character's inability to express what he thinks and feels. Without the demonstration there is no performance.

Do I need to read the entire script, since I have only a limited amount of time to prepare for the reading?

Yes, you should make every effort to get the entire script, and read it carefully. Information not included in your character's dialogue, or even in the scenes in which your character appears, might be all-important to the effectiveness of your reading in a number of ways.

First, the entire script will yield many more clues about the tone of the material than only one character's sides or scenes possibly could. The reason for that is that each character has his own point of view, whereas the entire script contains all the subjective viewpoints and compiles them in a way that best serves and presents the writer's vision. That vision can only be clearly understood by reading the complete text.

Second, if even one bit of vital character or situation information appears only in other characters' scenes and dialogue, your performance might be not only ineffective, but rendered completely inappropriate by your lack of that important insight.

How important are the words?

Very. First, because they tell how the character expresses himself—his manner of speech and the things (and the kinds of things) he feels it important to say. In many cases, speech is an important indicator of a character's mental, emotional, physical, spiritual, cultural, intellectual, or even his financial components. For these reasons, an actor would do well to investigate carefully the reasons that underlie a character's words before deciding he shouldn't say them.

The second reason for being careful about the words, and perhaps in a practical sense the most important, is that the writer might be in the room when you are reading for the part. Some writers are very protective about their words, and some writers don't care as long as the material works and the character works.

An actor should never make arbitrary dialogue changes, nor should he purposely change words without consulting the director. In an audition situation, the most direct approach an actor can take regarding word changes is to get the changes approved before he reads. Extending that simple courtesy in the casting session will accomplish a number of positive things. First, it will demonstrate the actor's respect for the writer's work and the director's authority. Second, it will create the impression that the actor makes reasoned choices, *but this will only be true if the actor's changes are minimal, specific, and supported by valid story and character considerations.* Third, dealing in specifics will help the actor to justify and solidify his choices. Finally, asking to change a word or two for specific and sensible reasons will indicate an important element of professionalism that makes producers and directors comfortable.

If the auditioning actor feels compelled to suggest word changes for his reading, there are many ways of approaching the subject tactfully. Here are two examples:

"I have a question. May I change two words in the script?"

or

"I have a question. Would it be all right if I added the word 'yes' at the end of the first speech?"

In most cases, they will okay the request without hesitation, and they will appreciate the fact that you asked.

How do I approach the part if there are only a few lines of dialogue?

Exactly the same way you would approach any other role. Your character isn't less of a person because he has only a few lines or because he doesn't appear much in the script. Jane Wyman and Holly Hunter both won best actress Academy Awards playing characters who *never* spoke.

What is the "point" of a line of dialogue?

The point of a line is the *character's intention* in that line.

To find the point of a line, paraphrase it *as concisely as possible* from the character's standpoint. For example, the line might read:

"We have a lot of ground to cover, and enemy infantry is all around us. They are the best marksmen in Europe."

But the point of the line is:

"Don't do anything stupid to get us killed."

By getting to the point of the line, you eliminate all the objectivity in it. It then has relevance to the character.

What are stage directions and narrative, and are they important to an actor in a cold reading?

The terms "stage directions" and "narrative" mean the same thing, but they are used in different contexts. "Stage directions" is a theatrical term referring to the unspoken portion of the play's text, which describes setting, the light and sound cues, and the action of the play. "Narrative" is the film and television equivalent of stage directions, which describes time, place, and action of the film, and, sometimes, the thoughts and feelings of the characters.

Stage directions and narrative are of critical importance to an actor's understanding of the material, and must be read and absorbed as carefully as the dialogue. In film and television scripts particularly, writers frequently use the narrative to illuminate nuances of character, and the actor would be well-advised to avail himself of whatever insights the writer has provided.

Even though it should go without saying, I will offer one piece of advice. In your earnest desire to assimilate the demands of your character, never take leave of your common sense. You must never attempt to accommodate the physical description of a character that does not and cannot apply to you, such as references to age, height, weight, ethnicity, eye color, hair color, and the like. Accept the fact that those items have already been changed in the minds of those who brought you in to read.

What is the "tone" of the script, and how might that affect my reading?

"Tone" refers to the approach or style of the material that is intended by the writer and the director. Melodramatic, farcical, theatrical, and documentary are examples of tone. The tone of a script is most governed by its believability. In some cases, the writer and the director are perfectly aware of the script's level of believability. Sometimes they are not.

The actor's only currency is the truth. For that reason, the believability of the material has no effect on the character because the character always accepts that he and his situation are real, and he will always behave truthfully in that universe. So the material's believability should have no impact upon your portrayal of the character.

But there is one adjustment the actor should make when the script's credibility is questionable: the adjustment is speed. Giving your character a reason to pick up the pace, thereby giving each moment less gravity, will actually make the material seem more real.

Regardless of the believability or unbelievability of the script, the actor should never "comment" on the material in the audition situation, either in the reading itself or in conversation. The only exception to this is the instances in which you *honestly* believe the material to be exceptionally good in some way, in which cases you should say so if given the opportunity.

How will I know what scenes I should audition with?

When you are given an appointment to read, you will be told the name of the character and, usually, you will be given a description of the character and his involvement in the story. The scenes you will be expected to read will be clearly marked in the material provided you.

In some cases, the scene or scenes the actor is asked to prepare are not the scenes that show the most interesting aspects of the character. In those cases, you should ask, as soon as you have read *all* the material, whether or not you may choose a particular scene or scenes that you feel will better demonstrate your ability to portray the character. The request should be straightforward, and it might be made in this way:

"I have a question. I have been asked to read scene 87 for the character of Dr. Jones. I think scene 74 shows more of what Dr. Jones is going through. May I read scene 74 instead of scene 87?"

Casting directors usually approve that kind of request. In the event you can't get an answer before the audition, then you should prepare both scenes and ask again in the audition session.

What should I do if I find a role in the script that seems better, and better suited to me, than the role I have been asked to read for?

You have to be especially careful about this one. Before you even consider approaching this subject, read *all* the material (the entire script) very carefully. Be absolutely sure that you understand all the aspects of the "other" role, so that you are perfectly confident that it is right for you.

Your first and most obvious consideration is the essence of the character. Know that you can convincingly play the character, and that you will be believable in that role in the context of the entire script.

Your second consideration is the character's importance in the script, relative to the importance of the role you have been asked to read for. Be sure that the role you want is significantly better than the role for which they are already considering you.

Finally, be aware of the industry's perception of the importance of the role you want. Even if you think there is a chance of the role being offered to someone with a bigger name, don't be deterred if you have a strong sense that the part is right for you. The time may be right for you to have that part, but you will have to convince "them." Be convincing enough and the part will be yours. One of my most rewarding experiences was playing the role of Herb Lee in *My Favorite Year.* I told Richard Benjamin, who was directing the picture, that I wanted very badly to play that part, not knowing that it had been offered to another actor. So even though I was being considered for another part, when the Herb Lee role became available, Richard offered it to me.

If you are certain that you want to read for something other than what they want you to read for, ask the casting director as soon as you finish reading the material and have decided that you want to play the other part. Your request might go something like this:

"I have a question. I'll be reading for the role of Senator Stevens, but I wondered if I might also read for FBI Agent Roberts? It's a part I feel very strongly about, and I think it's as right for me as the role of the senator is."

Notice that this approach doesn't negate the possibility of your playing the role they originally had you in mind for. If your request gets a negative response, drop it, and you've lost nothing. If you don't get an answer to your request before the reading, ask again in the audition. They might go for it.

Should I read with an accent or dialect if the script indicates that the character has one?

Only if you can do it perfectly. If you have presented yourself as a master of that particular accent or dialect, then do it. But it had better be good. Never put anything into your reading that is less than professional and perfect. Only do what you know that you do well in all aspects of your work, and endeavor to improve the other things in your private rehearsal time. Always being confident that your work is the best will ensure that it is.

Should I approach every script in the same way (and are there guidelines I can follow)?

Yes, it is a good idea to approach every script in the same way because the goal of achieving a complete, truthful performance is the same every time. This is the process (and the sequence) that works best for me:

1. Get as much of the script as you can, and read it thoroughly.
2. Use Situation Perception to isolate the key elements of the material and to identify those that are relevant to the reading.
3. Read the audition scenes for *complete* understanding.
4. Describe your character's essence (in one word if possible).
5. Define the concept of each scene in terms of the character's desire and expectation (they might not be the same).
6. Find the point of each line, and write it in the margin next to the line. Then reread the line several times with that intention. Let the emotions happen.
7. Reread the audition scenes several times to reinforce each moment and the progression from moment to moment.
8. Rehearse at performance level (with the same intensity you intend for the reading) to free yourself from the printed page. Continue to rehearse as much as time permits.

With Mare Winningham in the "Button, Button" episode of "The Twilight Zone."

Explaining haberdashery to Redd Foxx in "Sanford and Son."

As Longly in *Close Encounters of the Third Kind.*

Jason Robards gets a lesson in slant drilling in *Comes a Horseman.*

Working on the jogging scene in *Ordinary People* with Donald Sutherland and Robert Redford.

Mark Linn-Baker gives Herb's tea to Bill Macy in *My Favorite Year.*

Blake Edwards choreographs Ellen Barkin's knockout punch in *Switch*.

With Nicolas Coster, John Saxon and James B. Sikking in *The Electric Horseman*.

Pleading George Memmoli's case to Charles Haid in "Hill Street Blues."

Reading the riot act to Corey Haim in the *Double O Kid.*

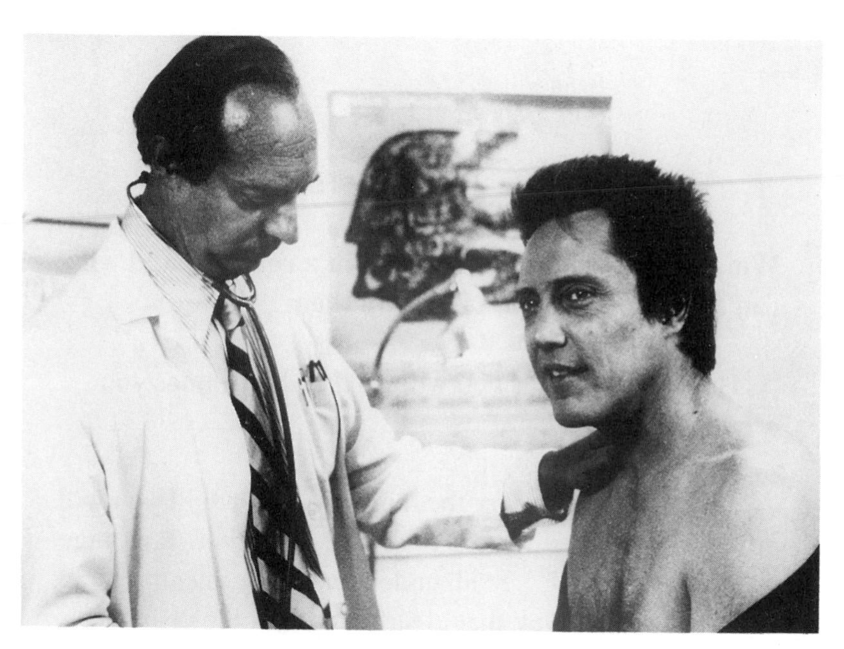

Christopher Walken's skeptical doctor in *Communion.*

Selling the political defense to Henry Winkler and Michael Keaton in *Night Shift.*

What *technical* skills will I need in a reading, and what can I do to develop and improve them?

These are the skills you will need and the things you need to do:

1. The first and by far the most important skill you will need is the ability to read the English language understandingly. To read understandingly means being able to read in a way that clearly conveys the character's message. In order to convey what the character means, you must understand what the character means. *Never, never, never read a single word of dialogue that you don't understand.* You must understand the dictionary meanings and the character's usage of *every* word. Giving an intelligent reading is the easiest task you have to perform, and it can't be faked. Your reading will either make sense, or it won't. The only person you will fool by reading something you don't understand is yourself. Except for dictionary definitions, the only source for information about intended meanings in the script is the script itself. If a careful reading of the material leaves certain meanings unclear, then use Situation Perception to analyze the key elements more specifically. If the script still doesn't yield the answer, you will need to put in a call to the casting department for clarification. Sometimes important details are lost in the rewriting process, in which case the answer you are looking for is in an earlier draft.

2. After you have made complete sense of the material, you must be able to read it feelingly, as it comes out of the

life of the character. The character's essence will underlie everything you do and say and the way that you do and say them. If you capture the character's essence, you will give your reading its most interesting and powerful element. Reading from the character's essence will actually guide the rest of your performance.

Besides reading from the character's essence, you must pay particular attention to the value you place on thought-bearing words, as all human beings do in conversation. Most especially, be aware of words that indicate absolutes, extremes, unusual conditions or situations, excitement, and horror. Words in these categories would include, respectively: "all" and "never," "huge" and "despondent," "one-eyed" and "flooded," "frenzied" and "sparkling," and "terrifying" and "decapitated." Your character will have a special intent in choosing words in those categories, so those words will have special value when he says them.

3. Let your character be surprised when confronted by the unexpected, even in a small degree. Unless your character has read the script (which he hasn't), there will be surprises that he isn't prepared for. Make him deal with them. He must behave as real people behave.

4. Read facing forward as much as possible, which means placing the person with whom you are reading facing you with his back to the audience. The people auditioning you will want to see as much of your face as possible, so they will probably already have the audition situation set up in that way. If the chair placement has you too much in profile (or is unsuitable in some other way), ask to change it. They will want you to be the best you can be.

5. Always read seated, unless you feel there is some particular physicality that you need to display by standing.

6. Choose a hard, uncomfortable chair to sit in if one is available. Otherwise, sit on the edge of the chair while reading. Never sit full into a comfortable chair in a reading. It will take away a substantial part of your energy.

7. Read off the page. Make eye contact with the person who is reading with you. Draw that person into the scene. It will make your reading more real because the character's experience will become more important than the actor's experience. Practice reading ahead so that you can begin and end each sentence without looking at the script. This is a skill you can only attain with practice, and you will attain it with practice.

8. Maintain the eye contact when the other person is reading. The people you are auditioning for will want to see your truthful facial reactions.

9. Use your free hand to mark your place in the script while you are looking up. With practice, you will find a comfortable technique for yourself. Keeping a finger on the script will relieve you of any impulse you might have to make meaningless gestures. Hold the script high enough so that you can refer to it with a minimum of head bobbing (preferably none), but not so high that it blocks your face.

10. On that extremely rare occasion when you know that you have allowed yourself to become unfocused in a reading, *stop immediately* (and fearlessly and unapologetically) and ask to begin again. A simple "May we start again?" will suffice. Never go as far as a page into the reading and attempt to start over. The best and most professional course of action is to concentrate and focus on

your assignment before you get into the audition room so that you are undistractable.

How can an acting coach help my reading?

A good acting coach can be invaluable to you if you find yourself facing a particularly troublesome role, and you have limited time to work it out. The coach will help you by quickly defining the problem and giving you a specific solution, in terms you can understand and easily assimilate. Besides dealing with what you regard as a problem, a coach should be able to reinforce the entire compass of the reading. In the course of working on the specifics of a particular reading, a good coach will also give you an understanding of the process involved, so that what you learn about playing the current character gives you insights you will use in playing future roles.

If you feel that the periodic use of an acting coach would be helpful to you, then you need to find a coach whose personality you find acceptable and whose acting concepts work for you. Because you are in the acting profession, you require a coach who is an experienced professional actor or director (preferably an actor). Otherwise, you put yourself in the position of trusting that your coach has the ability to imagine the acting experience without ever having personally gone through it himself.

Once you've made the decision to work with a coach, and having found a good coach who helps you achieve the results you need, stay with him. Use his coaching to strengthen your own techniques, so that he will be challenged by your growth to demand more from you. Make your muscles remember everything they learn.

How should I dress for the reading?

Dress appropriately for the character, but not necessarily for the scenes you are reading. For example, the character is a high-powered attorney, and the scenes you will be reading are in the family bedrooms. You would be better advised to wear a business suit than a robe and slippers. Surgical gowns and evening dresses are virtually never appropriate for readings. Give the people who are auditioning you credit for being able to visualize some things, particularly wardrobe changes and period costumes. Your own common sense will be a great help in this.

How much makeup should I wear in a reading?

As little as possible to be appropriate to the character. For men, this usually means none.

Should I use props in a reading?

Only minimally. If you can do the reading with no props, it is even better. Actors rarely use props in readings, and they are not expected to. For those reasons, any props you use will call attention to themselves. If you use them less than naturally and expertly, the focus (yours and that of those who are watching you) will shift irretrievably from the important matter of acting to your lack of dexterity. While you think they are paying attention to your reading, they will, instead, be wondering what possessed you to handicap your own performance. Furthermore, you will make them uncomfortable, which will not only lose the job but will make it difficult to convince them to see you again.

If you have a specific and wonderful reason to use a particular prop, and you use it well, the element of surprise will work in your favor. But both conditions must prevail if props are to have any positive effect in a reading. There must be some compelling reason to use them, and you must use them well. Otherwise, don't push your luck.

What is a callback, and how should I prepare for it?

A callback is a second (or third, or fourth, etc.) reading for the same production and, usually, for the same role.

Unless you are given specific instructions to the contrary, do everything in the callback *exactly* as you did them in the previous reading. And dress exactly the same way. They called you back because they liked something they saw. If you change something, you might be changing the thing they want to see again. Darrell Royal, a very successful football coach at the University of Texas, was asked by a reporter, after the team had won the Southwest Conference championship, whether he would change his game plan for the Cotton Bowl on New Year's Day. Royal's answer got right to the point. "Nope. We'll dance with who brung us." Don't argue with success.

How should I regard other actors in the waiting room?

With politeness and silence. You are on a mission and must not be distracted. Do not engage other actors in conversation. Ideally, you should find a place where you can concentrate (and work aloud when necessary).

Be aware that some actors' standard mode of operation is to be conversational, funny (they think), loud, boastful, or distracting in some other way designed to destroy the concentration of other actors. Don't do it, and don't fall for it or accept it when other actors try to do it to you. Even if it's someone you *need* to have a conversation with, don't do it; get a phone number and call him later. Every actor in the waiting room knows that every other actor is waiting to read, so *any* anti-concentration behavior should be regarded as hostile. If anyone tries to prolong conversation with you beyond a simple greeting, cut it off quickly. You might try something like this:

"Can you stay around for a while? Let's talk when I come out."

Then go right back to the script. Do not try to assess the experience, success, wealth, state of preparedness, relative appropriateness for the part you are reading for, or any aspect of the other actors in the waiting room. None of that has anything to do with you, and it can only diffuse your confidence and your concentration.

If, for any reason, there are too many distractions in the waiting room, find out when the casting director will be ready for you, then get out. Give yourself those precious extra minutes of concentration somewhere else, and then come back when they're ready for your reading.

Your reading will succeed only if you are prepared *and maintain your preparedness.* Don't be distracted. Stay focused.

Are there necessities common to every reading situation?

Yes. Even though each reading presents a new experience, there are important commonalities that must be dealt with in the same way every time. Here is a checklist of the necessities:

1. Be thoroughly prepared so that every moment of your reading will have clarity and assuredness. Use as much rehearsal time as possible to accomplish this. Being completely prepared will give you the flexibility to react in character to the unexpected.
2. Know who you will be reading for. Neither the number of people in the audition room nor their identities should surprise you. It is particularly important that you greet people by name if you have met them previously.
3. Begin concentrating on the reading before you enter the audition room, and stay focused when you enter. Allow nothing to distract you: not conversation, not phone calls, not inattentiveness, not rudeness, not body language, not a bad reading by the casting assistant, nothing.
4. Be pleasant and businesslike, and let them know by your demeanor that you are ready to do the work.

5. Do not act. You are the character, and you have the character's perception of the situation. That is the only reality. Let it unfold truthfully and surprisingly moment-by-moment.

6. Thank them and leave, exuding the same confidence you came in with.

Will they give me direction before I read?

Not if you can stop them. Unless you have specific questions about the material, gently resist their inclination to direct you before the fact (except in the case of television commercials). Usually a director's pre-audition direction is meant to be helpful, but the result of it might not be. Even though you have assiduously prepared for the reading, you may, in your desire to please the director, be vulnerable to the one suggestion that will dismantle the entire foundation of your performance. Acting is such a subjective experience that actors frequently destroy their well-prepared readings because they misunderstand pre-audition directions, when the director might have been thrilled to see what the actors had come up with on their own.

Before I read for the role of Drollhauser, the attorney in *Night Shift,* Ron Howard, who is a very good director, offered to give me his concept of the character. I respectfully declined because I felt confident with my preparation, and I didn't want to discard it out of an obligation to give him my split-second rendition of his version. And besides, he could always give me his direction after seeing what I had to offer. Also, it was important to me that Ron have some idea of the kind of work he could expect me to bring to the set if he hired me to play the part (which he did). As it turned out, he liked my reading. But if he hadn't liked it, he would still have had the option to direct me, and I would have had the opportunity to demonstrate my ability to take direction.

There are actors who want to hear everything a director has to say, even before they read. It is their belief that the more information they have, the better they will be, and they also believe that it works for them. Nevertheless, most directors want to see what the actor does before they direct him. If you come to a reading (or a job) expecting the director to lead you, you will be in for a shock. And you and the director will be deprived of some original magic that might have come out of you. The actor's most powerful creative tools are his instincts, and no director wants to take those away from him.

Will they like me?

What do you care? You are not there to win their approval. You are there to help them out of a problem. That is the powerful subtext underlying the audition situation. They have a part and no actor to play it. This is an unpleasant experience for them, and they would rather be somewhere else. Anywhere. You can show them who that character is. Give them that person in the script, and they can all go home. You will have solved their problem, and they will feel much better after you leave the room than they did before you walked in.

Then they will like you.

When is it all right to ask questions in a reading?

When you have questions that *need* to be answered, ask them before you read. And only if the answers will affect your reading. Never ask questions that have nothing to do with the material before you read. And never leave necessary questions about the material unasked.

If there are several people in the room, how will I know which person I'll be reading with?

If it isn't perfectly obvious, ask. It goes like this:

"I have a question. Who am I reading with?"

It may seem like an insignificant point, but it's not. Many a role has been lost because a little surprise at the beginning of the reading destroyed the actor's concentration.

What should I do if the person I'm reading with isn't a good reader?

The first thing you need to do is forget that it's a reading. You must regard the person you are reading with (the reader) as the character, or characters in the script, and you must see him through the eyes of your character. Then you will be free to react in character to everything he says and does. The way he reads will become nothing more than that character's speech pattern.

What do directors mean when they say, "Make it bigger"?

Bigger seldom means bigger—it is usually shorthand for something else. It usually means that they want it clearer. It almost never means that they want it less truthful, but frequently more so. The next time you are asked to make the work bigger, be sure that what you are doing and saying is crystal clear *in the character's mind.* Then when you do it again it will be bigger.

There will be cases in which the director will want your work to be bigger just to satisfy some stylistic concept, but those times will be rare. Bigness in and of itself is meaningless, and may actually be counterproductive to the effect you're trying to achieve. Several years ago, I was in a production of *South Pacific* in New York at Jones Beach Theatre, with a seating capacity of 8,200, more than four times the size of most Broadway theaters. After several weeks of performances, I gradually found myself trying to compensate for the size of the house by making my performance "bigger." It was absurd. The theater was so big and the distance from the stage so great that only the people in the first few rows could even see the actors' facial expressions with any clarity. So, for the people who could see me clearly, my performance had become grotesque. For the others, it made little difference. When I came to my senses and behaved like a real person, I'm sure my performance was more satisfactory for the entire audience. It had to be.

What do directors mean when they say, "Bring it down," or "It's over the top"?

When you are asked to bring it down or pull it in, you are probably being asked tactfully to make it more real. A "big" performance that is truthful can be effective, no matter how realistic the tone of the material may be. If you doubt this, I refer you to the careers of such actors as Kirk Douglas, Bette Davis, George C. Scott, Al Pacino, and Jack Nicholson.

Sometimes an actor will allow his insecurity or nervousness about a role to propel him beyond what otherwise might have been pretty good work. In such a case, a simple reminder to bring it down might be helpful. When I did my first movie, *Lady Liberty,* I was nervous about a scene I had to do with Sophia Loren, who was a major international star (and unbelievably beautiful). It was a night shoot at John F. Kennedy Airport in New York City, and we had worked on the scene all evening and into the wee hours of the morning. I didn't notice that my nervous energy level was edging higher as the evening progressed. The crew was almost finished setting the lights for my closeup at the point where I have an angry confrontation with Sophia. She was sitting fewer than two feet away, smiling at me, and she did a very kind thing. Sophia spoke to me, sweetly and simply. She said, "Do less." I'll never forget it. It was the best acting note I had ever gotten, because it was so succinct and correct and understandable.

If you are asked to make your reading smaller, your first thought should be about the truthfulness of your work. If you are in the life of the person you are playing, the work will, of necessity, be lifelike. Life is what it is. But if you are faking the work, doing less won't help. You can't improve a big, empty performance by making it smaller. You will only wind up with a tiny, empty performance.

What is a beat?

A beat is a short (usually a second or two) wait between acting moments. The expression is thought to have originated when a German director in Hollywood referred to a "bit" (which sounded like "beat") of time that he wanted to lapse before the actor spoke his next line. The term always sounds a little mechanical to me, so I prefer to use the word "moment."

If I am directed to do the scene faster or slower or bigger or smaller or louder or quieter how can I make that quick adjustment without being artificial?

Regardless of how mechanical the direction seems, your adjustment must always be organic. The only way to achieve that is to make it the character's problem and not the actor's problem.

When you make character choices, as all of your acting choices should be, the options are virtually infinite. Here are a few examples:

1. "Make it faster."

   You are excited about something.
   You have an urgent need to impart information.
   You have an important appointment in fifteen minutes.

2. "Make it slower."
    You need to make sure that they understand every point.
    You don't feel comfortable about saying it.
    You are not feeling well.
3. "Make it bigger."
    You are losing your patience.
    You are overjoyed.
    The other characters are very young.
4. "Make it smaller."
    The situation is intimate.
    The information is confidential.
    The room is small.
5. "Make it louder."
    There is a lot of background noise.
    What you have to say is very important.
    The other characters aren't paying attention.
6. "Make it quieter."
    You are ashamed of what you are saying.
    You don't want to attract attention.
    You are dying.

If you have studied the material, your character's options will be clear. You will be able to respond quickly to direction, and the results will be truthful and surprising.

What should I do if, after I read, they ask me to read for another part that I haven't prepared?

To begin with, when those who will make the actual hiring decision want to see more of you, they have given you some important information. They have told you, without saying it directly, that your essence fits into their concept of the project and that your reading captured what they intended as the tone of the material. Knowing this should give you a confidence boost as you go to the next step. You should also know that asking you to read for a different role does not rule out the possibility that they will hire you to play the role you originally read for. It only means that they liked what they saw but they think you might be better suited for something different. They are in the process of working it out.

When you are asked to read for another part, you will be asked if you need some time to prepare it. Always take as much time as they are willing to give you (if you need the time and intend to use it). If for some reason they don't ask if you need time, and it will be very unusual if they don't, you must ask for it. They expect you to ask for time to prepare. The amount of time you will have to study the new role will depend on the project, the importance of the part, and the production schedule. For important roles in some projects, you may be given a day or longer. In most instances, they will expect you to take from a few minutes to an hour, and, in most instances, that will be enough time, particularly since you will probably already have some familiarity with the character from your previous work on the material.

One final note on this subject: if your previous reading of the material left you confused in any way about the character you have now been asked to read, you should ask whatever questions you have before you leave the room. If you have already left the audition room with the script (or sides) and new questions arise, you will have to have them answered, if you can, before you go back in to read. Tell the casting director (or casting assistant or receptionist) that you have a question. You might ask like this:

"Excuse me. I have a question. Can you tell me if Sam is Amanda's father? The script doesn't seem to make it clear."

Asking the question in this way will get you the answer you need without making it appear that you are criticizing the material. If you have questions that haven't been answered before you return to read, then ask in the audition room. Never audition with material that you don't understand.

What should I do if I get a wonderful idea about the character or the scene after I've left the audition room?

If you feel very strongly about it, and you know that your second reading would be substantially different, then *privately* tell the casting director, casting assistant, or receptionist. If they ask you to read again, wonderful. If not, leave and forget about it.

You must know that many, if not most, actors always think they can do it better the next time. The work will never be perfect, but there will always be a time when the performance will count, perfect or not. This is why the preparation process is so important.

How do I get readings for commercials?

With the exception of those instances where actors are requested by directors and producers, casting directors make the decisions about which actors get to read for commercials. So it is important to meet the casting directors. Their names and phone numbers are available through Screen Actors Guild and in publications available at bookstores that service the entertainment industry.

Unlike the casting procedure for plays, movies, and television shows, casting calls for commercials are always placed through agents. And agents in the commercial industry also have the opportunity to secure more audition appointments for their talent than is true for agents in other acting fields, probably because of the greater number of actors who are auditioned for each role. For that reason, an actor who wants to work in television commercials should call the agents who represent actors in that industry. (In Los Angeles, agents only represent actors who sign contracts for exclusive representation. In New York, some agents work with free-lance actors.) Agent information is available from the same sources that provide casting director information.

Regardless of the relative importance of agents in commercials, the actor who is known by the casting director has a better chance of getting an audition appointment than if he is not known. Agents only submit their talent as casting suggestions, and that is where their power stops.

Will I have the copy in advance?

Probably not. It is a good idea to get to the audition at least half an hour before your appointment time, to familiarize yourself with the copy. And use the time for that. Other less profitable uses for your time will appear. Don't use them.

What do I do if they want to direct me before I read?

Be grateful and attentive. Unlike all other acting situations, the actor in commercials is secondary to the product and the mechanics of the scene. The actor's performance has to fit into strict constraints of time and space. Those will be explained in detail, and if anything is unclear, ask for more details. Be especially clear about where they want you to look.

Don't allow the mechanical aspect of the setup to influence the honesty of your performance. Your reading must contain all the elements of truthful acting that are demanded in any other reading situation. The more information you get about the concept and the camera shot and its logistical requirements, the more you will be able to forget them and play the scene.

What do I need to know about using the cue card?

Whenever there are lines for the actor to speak, a cue card will be in the audition room.

If you are the only actor in the scene, then you may ask for the card to be placed closest to where you will be expected to look most of the time, and your request will usually be accommodated. If you have a lot of copy to read, then you must decide where you will look, and be firm about it. Do not allow your eyes to drift around while you figure out whether you should be looking at the cue card or the camera lens or some other place. If you can make gestures and glances an organic part of your reading, then you can look at the lens part of the time and at the cue card at other times. If you can't comfortably pick up your lines and then go back to the camera, then you must find the spot closest to the camera for your eyeline, from where you can also read the lines.

If a cue card is provided for the audition, do I have to use it?

No. But the only reason not to use the cue card is that your audition will be better if you don't use it. Even though use of the cue card has become standard in the commercial industry, some actors aren't comfortable reading from it. Also, the cue card is sometimes placed in a position that makes its use awkward and unnatural.

If you aren't able to read comfortably from the cue cards, or you can't find the camera lens and your lines on the cue card at the same time when it is required, then you must find another way. There are two options.

If you can get to the audition early enough, you might want to memorize your lines. Memorizing commercial copy is easy in most cases because the actors usually don't have many lines.

When there is too much copy to memorize, your other option is to take the script into the audition with you and read from that. You may get some initial resistance from the video-camera operator running the audition, but it won't be much if you explain that you can't see the cue card.

As in all reading situations, you, the actor, are in charge. You must frame the audition experience in a way that works best for you. Everybody involved wants you to be as good as you can be.

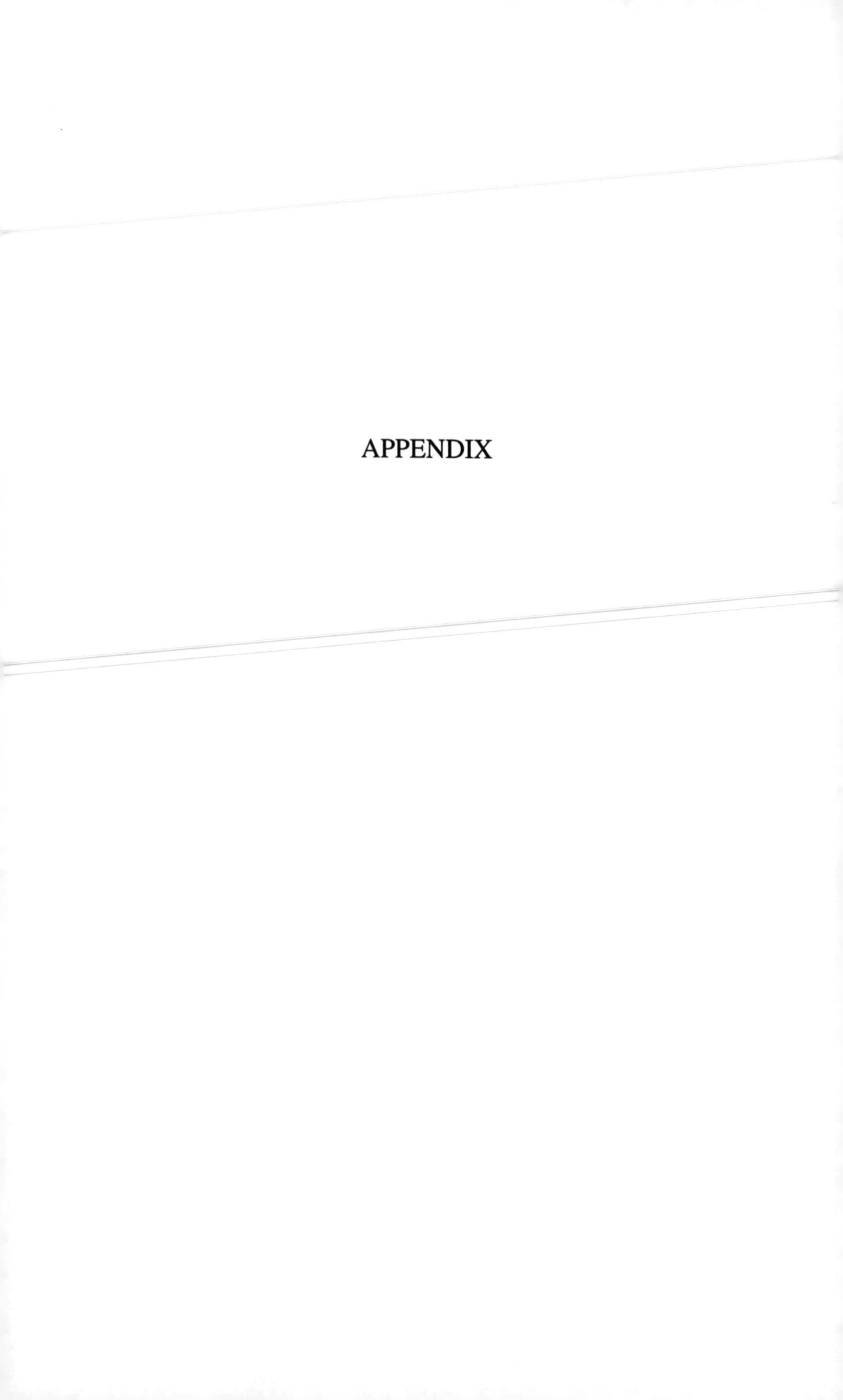

APPENDIX

ABOUT THE AUTHOR

Basil Hoffman is an actor whose film career has spanned more than two decades, beginning with Mario Monicelli's *Lady Liberty,* starring Sophia Loren, in 1972. His more than two dozen films include some of the best known work of directors such as Richard Benjamin, Ron Howard, Carl Reiner, Blake Edwards, Alan J. Pakula, and Academy Award winners Stanley Donen, Steven Spielberg, Delbert Mann, Sydney Pollack, and Robert Redford. Those films include *All the President's Men, Close Encounters of the Third Kind, Comes a Horseman, Switch, The Electric Horseman, The Milagro Beanfield War, Night Shift, My Favorite Year,* Academy Award winning Best Picture *Ordinary People,* and many others.

On television, he has appeared in numerous mini-series and films, and more than 80 series episodes including multiple appearances in "M*A*S*H," "Sanford and Son," "Marcus Welby, M.D.," "Dynasty," and others. For two years he played the recurring role of Ed Greenglass in "Hill Street Blues." He was a series regular in CBS' "Square Pegs" as Principal Dingleman.

His stage performances include *South Pacific* at Jones Beach and more than 20 productions in stock and off Broadway. His Los Angeles theater credits include the award-winning production of Romulus Linney's *Sand Mountain* for which he won a Drama-Logue award, the West Coast premiere of Lanford Wilson's *Serenading Louie,* and the world premiere of *Walking Peoria,* by William Blinn.

He has been an actor and spokesman in more than 250 television commercials.

Mr. Hoffman is a private acting coach and has conducted seminars and lectured on the subjects of acting, the business of acting, the screenwriter and the actor, and careers in film at UCLA; the University of Southern California; California State University, Northridge; Tulane University; Emerson College; The American

Academy of Dramatic Arts; Paramount Studios; and the American Film Institute.

Mr. Hoffman is a corporate presentation and media consultant, and teaches effective American speech to foreign speakers. He has prepared attorneys and their clients for trials and government hearings (including the highly publicized and televised U.S. Senate Government Affairs Committee campaign finance hearings in Washington D.C. in October, 1997).

Mr. Hoffman is a former member of the board of directors of Screen Actors Guild and the President's Fine Arts Advisory Council of Loyola Marymount University. He is a member of the board of trustees of the American Academy of Dramatic Arts and a member of the board of directors of the Salvatori Center for Service Learning at the University of Southern California. He has been a member of the Academy of Motion Picture Arts and Sciences since 1978.

Mr. Hoffman is a graduate of Tulane University (BBA) and the American Academy of Dramatic Arts.

Biographical references on Mr. Hoffman are included in *Who's Who in Entertainment,* beginning with the 2nd edition, *Halliwell's Filmgoer's Companion,* beginning with the 8th edition, and *Who's Who in America,* beginning with the 53rd edition.

All inquiries regarding the author should be directed to:
Lemack & Company Public Relations/Management
292 South La Cienega Boulevard, Suite 217
Beverly Hills, CA 90211
Phone 310/659-6300

FROM THE CRITICS

My Favorite Year—

". . . Basil Hoffman says one line aloud in the entire movie, and in a script loaded with better throw-away lines than most comedies can muster for their bombshells, the moment is one of the best."

Betsa Marsh
Cincinnati Enquirer

Comes a Horseman—

". . . fine performances by Basil Hoffman as George the Geologist who can think only in terms of oil, and by George Grizzard as his steely-eyed boss."

Richard Freedman
Newark, New Jersey *Sun Ledger*

Walking Peoria—

". . . the writer-director, Raymond Poole (the incomparable character actor Basil Hoffman), belongs to that peculiar Hollywood breed of hacks with thin skins."

"Key to the show's success is Hoffman, whose unforgettably deadpan portrayal suggests a Walking Burbank. With his protruding eyes and hound-dog face, the actor nurtures a terrific comic presence marked by impeccable timing. But he mines the character's flinty pathos as well, especially in a sharply written closing speech about betrayal."

Scott Collins
Los Angeles Times

ACKNOWLEDGMENTS

To Beulah and Dave for their unconditional love and support.

To Clifford Jackson for believing I could do it.

To Beth Allen for wanting 75 pictures.

To the following Hollywood casting directors who defied convention to give a new actor in town without an agent a chance to work: Bill Batliner, Phil Benjamin, Hoyt Bowers, Ross Brown, Reuben Cannon, Sam Christensen, Ruth Conforte, Dianne Crittenden, Joe D'Agosta, Pam Dixon, Rachelle Farberman, Jane Feinberg, Mike Fenton, Eddie Foy III, Phyllis Glick, Sylvia Gold, Millie Gusse, Milt Hammerman, Mike Hanks, Pat Harris, Tom Jennings, Marilyn Howard, Bill Kenny, Marsha Kleinman, Barbara Lawrence, Don McElwaine, Dodie McLean, Jim Merrick, Burt Metcalfe, Bob Morones, Claire Newell, Meryl O'Loughlin, Al Onorato, Marvin Paige, Tom Palmer, Pam Polifroni, Sally Powers, Joe Reich, Marvin Schnall, Bill Shepard, Joel Thurm, Beth Uffner, Renee Valente, Geri Windsor.

To the industry's best producers, directors, writers, and casting directors who have hired me and put me in the company of high standards.

To Alan Shayne, Alan J. Pakula and Robert Redford for *All the President's Men* and everything that followed.

To Brad Lemack and Stephen Calamita for years of loyalty.

To Roger Karshner for urging me to write this book.

To Christine for so much.

To God who makes it all possible.